C000125793

Table of Contents

Table of Contents

THIS IS THE ARSENAL PREMIER LEAGUE QUIZBOOK

The Quizbook is intended to take you through the Premier League years of Arsenal Football Club. (Everything is correct at date of writing July 2023)

It starts with the formation of the Premier League in 1992 in rough chronology through to the present day.

The book includes sections of multiple-choice questions in blocks of 10. In between the multiple-choice questions there are a variety of other questions I have put together in slightly different formats.

You will be asked to name the player, name those that crossed the divide, remember as many players as possible in some of Arsenals FA Cup triumphs. Some of them will take time and need to be thought about. If you take time to test your memory you will be rewarded

Each section can be cross referenced against the answers provided towards the end of the book.

Grab a drink, something to eat and a pencil and enjoy the quizbook – or take it to your friends and fill out together – or quiz your best mate who claims to know everything about Arsenal and see how much they truly know.

Most of all – enjoy and remember the thrilling Premier League seasons the Gunners have provided.

B DEMURE

Arsenal Premier League Years Quizbook

Premier League Years 1992-1995

1. Who was the Arsenal manager during the first
   season of the Premier League?

   a. Bruce Rioch ☐

   b. George Graham ☐

   c. Pat Rice ☐

   d. Stewart Houston ☐

2. Which player did Arsenal re-sign from Everton for a fee of £3 million having sold him for £1 million 3 years earlier?

    a. Steve Morrow ☐

    b. David Hillier ☐

    c. Martin Keown ☐

    d. Perry Groves ☐

3. Arsenal won the League Cup on 19th April 1993 beating Sheffield Wednesday 2-1 at Wembley. Paul Merson scored the first goal. But who scored the winning goal on 68 minutes?

    a. Steve Morrow ☐

    b. Ian Wright ☐

    c. Alan Smith ☐

    d. Ray Parlour ☐

4. Arsenal met Sheffield Wednesday again in the FA Cup final. The first game finished 1-1 meaning a replay was played on 20th May. All square at full time the match was won in extra time. What was the final score?

   a. 3-2 ☐

   b. 1-0 ☐

   c. 3-1 ☐

   d. 2-1 ☐

5. Ian Wright finished the season as Arsenals top goal scorer in the 1992-1993 season. He scored 15 league goals. But how many goals did he score in total including league and cup matches?

   a. 22 ☐

   b. 25 ☐

   c. 30 ☐

   d. 34 ☐

6. Having won the FA cup Arsenal qualified for the Cup Winners Cup. Undefeated on their run to the final and beating PSG in the semi final who did Arsenal defeat 1-0 in the final in Copenhagen on 4th May 1994?

   a. Parma ☐

   b. Ajax ☐

   c. Standard Liege ☐

   d. Torino ☐

7. In March 1994 which player left the club to join Everton following the arrival of Eddie McGoldrick?

   a. Ian Selley ☐

   b. Ray Parlour ☐

   c. Anders Limpar ☐

   d. Paul Dickov ☐

8. On January 1st 1995 Arsenal signed 19 year old Welsh Striker John Hartson for £3.75m from which club?

    a. Luton Town ☐

    b. Swansea City ☐

    c. Norwich City ☐

    d. Cardiff City ☐

9. Despite a disappointing 1994-95 season finishing 12th in the league which player scored 18 league goals?

    a. John Hartson ☐

    b. Chris Kiwomya ☐

    c. Ian Wright ☐

    d. Paul Merson ☐

10. Arsenal looked to defend their Cup Winners Cup trophy in the 1994/95 season. Ultimately ending in disappointment with a Final defeat against Real Zaragoza. Who scored an extra time winner in the 119th minute?

    a. Gustavo Poyet ☐

    b. Nayim ☐

    c. Juan Esnaider ☐

    d. Geli ☐

(ANSWERS CAN BE FOUND ON PAGE 82)

SECTION TWO

NAME THE FAMOUS GOONERS

1. Signed for a fee of £7.1 million from Sampdoria in July 1995. A regular England international who scored 27 goals in 62 games for his country.

2 Played 558 league games for Arsenal between 1975 and 1993. Who is this Republic of Ireland international?

3 Who is the 'Romford Pele?' he still holds the record for most Premier League appearances with 333.

```
[                                    ]
```

4 In 2008 this player became the youngest Arsenal player to appear on the European stage when he came on as a sub at just 16 years 329 days old.

```
[                                    ]
```

5 This Russian was the most expensive player in Arsenal history when he signed for £15 million in the 08-09 winter transfer window.

```
[                                    ]
```

6 At just 17 years old this player signed for Arsenal from PSG for £500,000 in February 1997. He scored 28 goals for Arsenal before departing to join Real Madrid for £22 million in 1999.

---

7 In 1999 this Arsenal youth player made his Arsenal debut in a league cup game against Middlesbrough. He made over 200 appearances for his boyhood club before departing in acrimonious circumstances joining Chelsea in 2006.

---

8 Originally signed as a back up to the answer for number 7 this left back signed from French club Cannes as a teenager in 2003. He made 264 appearances for the club before joining Manchester City in 2011 for £7 million.

---

9 At just 16 years old this player signed for Arsenal from Southampton in 2006. The pacy winger went on to play nearly 400 games for Arsenal scoring over 100 goals.

```
[                                    ]
```

10 English centre-back. Joined Arsenal on a free transfer from Tottenham Hotspur in 2001. He won the Premier League twice with Arsenal and the FA cup on 3 occasions.

```
[                                    ]
```

(ANSWERS CAN BE FOUND ON PAGE 83)

SECTION THREE

ARSENAL
1993 FA CUP FINAL XI

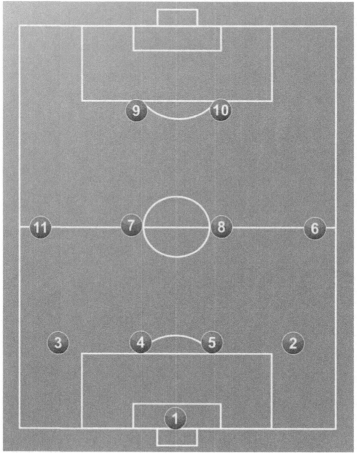

(The numbers used are to represent positions only – they are not accurate as worn on the day)

How many of the Arsenal 1993 FA CUP winning starting XI can you name? Initials used to give you a helping hand:

1. DS	
2. LD	
3. NW	
4. AL	
5. TA	
6. PD	
7. JJ	
8. IW	
9. KC	
10. PM	
11. RP	

(ANSWERS CAN BE FOUND ON PAGE 84)

SECTION FOUR

ARSENAL PREMIER LEAGUE YEARS 1996-1999

1. In 1996 Arsenal re-signed a veteran Goalkeeper from Leeds as back up. He had played over 200 games for Arsenal during the 1980s – who was he?

    a. Stuart Taylor ☐

    b. Jens Lehmann ☐

    c. Vince Bartram ☐

    d. John Lukic ☐

2. In September 1996 Arsene Wenger was unveiled as Arsenal manager leaving Japanese team Grampus Eight. What French club did he manage prior to heading to Japan?

    a. Monaco ☐

    b. Paris St Germain ☐

    c. Marseille ☐

    d. Toulouse ☐

3. Prior to Wengers arrival Arsenal signed two French midfielders – Arsenal are said to have completed the deals at his request. Who were the two players?

    a. Glenn Helder and Nicholas Anelka ☐

    b. Patrick Vieira and Remi Garde ☐

    c. Emmanuel Petit and Robert Pires ☐

    d. Gilles Grimandi and Kaba Diawara ☐

4. The 1997-98 season was Wengers first full season in charge. Arsenal went on to win the title with Manchester United finishing 2nd. How many points ahead were Arsenal at the end of the season?

    a. 1 ☐

    b. 3 ☐

    c. 5 ☐

    d. 7 ☐

5. Marc Overmars signed for Arsenal on 1st July 1997. The Dutch international scored 12 goals in the title winning season. Which club did he sign from in the previous summer?

    a. Willem II ☐

    b. Ajax ☐

    c. Barcelona ☐

    d. PSV ☐

6. Overmars scored the opening goal of the FA Cup final on 16th May 1998. Who did Arsenal Defeat 2-0 at Wembley to lift the cup?

   a. Leicester City ☐

   b. Chelsea ☐

   c. Cardiff City ☐

   d. Newcastle United ☐

7. In 1998 Arsenal signed a Swedish 21-year-old. Arsenal had scouted the player for over a year, but Wenger made the final decision to sign him after watching him impress on TV against England

   a. Freddie Ljungberg ☐

   b. Rami Shaaban ☐

   c. Stefan Schwartz ☐

   d. Sebastian Larsson ☐

8. Nwankwo Kanu signed for Arsenal in January 1999. He cost a fee around £4.5 million from which club did he sign?

   a. Ajax ☐

   b. Inter Milan ☐

   c. Portsmouth ☐

   d. West Bromwich Albion ☐

9. Which player finished top goalscorer for Arsenal at the end of the 1998-99 season? With 19 goals in all competitions

    a. Dennis Bergkamp ☐

    b. Marc Overmars ☐

    c. Nicholas Anelka ☐

    d. Nwankwo Kanu ☐

10. The 1998-99 season saw Arsenal finish second in the league and failing to defend their title despite it going all the way to the last game of the season. Who finished one point ahead of Arsenal?

    a. Leeds ☐

    b. Liverpool ☐

    c. Chelsea ☐

    d. Manchester United ☐

(ANSWERS CAN BE FOUND ON PAGE 85)

SECTION FIVE

ARSENAL PREMIER LEAGUE YEARS 2000-2003

1. The 1999-2000 season saw the arrival of one of the greatest players ever to wear an Arsenal shirt. How many league goals did Thierry Henry score in his debut season?

    a. 12 ☐

    b. 15 ☐

    c. 17 ☐

    d. 21 ☐

2. The 1999-2000 season saw a disappointing Champions League campaign as Arsenal dropped into the UEFA cup after the group stage. How did Arsenals UEFA cup run end?

    a. Winners ☐

    b. Runners up ☐

    c. Semi Final ☐

    d. Quarter Final ☐

3. In the summer of 2000 both Marc Overmars and Emmanuel Petit departed Highbury – where was their destination?

    a. Barcelona ☐

    b. Real Madrid ☐

    c. Bayern Munich ☐

    d. Paris Saint-Germain ☐

4. On Boxing day 2020 Thierry Henry scored his first hattrick for Arsenal in the Premier League. How many hattricks did Henry go on to score before departing Arsenal?

    a. 5 ☐

    b. 8 ☐

    c. 10 ☐

    d. 11 ☐

5. Arsenal signed a 20-year-old forward from Everton in 2001 for a fee in the region of £10 million. A disappointing spell in North London meant a return on loan to Everton a few years later before departing permanently to Charlton in 2004 who was he?

    a. Christopher Wreh ☐

    b. Graham Barrett ☐

    c. Danny Cadamarteri ☐

    d. Francis Jeffers ☐

6. 2001-2002 saw Arsenal complete a famous double. Which combination did they complete?

    a. Premier League and League Cup ☐

    b. Premier League and FA Cup ☐

    c. FA Cup and League Cup ☐

    d. FA Cup and Champions League ☐

7. Two Arsenal legends retired at the end of the 2001-2002 season. Tony Adams and which other player?

    a. Lee Dixon ☐

    b. Nigel Winterburn ☐

    c. Ray Parlour ☐

    d. David Seaman ☐

8. Arsene Wenger was awarded Manager of the Year in 2002. Which player won the Player of the year award?

    a. Thierry Henry ☐

    b. Robert Pires ☐

    c. Freddie Ljungberg ☐

    d. Dennis Bergkamp ☐

9. August 2002 saw Arsenal win the FA Community Shield 1-0 against Liverpool. Who scored the winning goal on their debut?

    a. Jermaine Pennant ☐

    b. Pascal Cygan ☐

    c. Giovanni Van Bronckhorst ☐

    d. Gilberto Silva ☐

10. The 2002-2003 season ended on a high for Arsenal when they won their ninth FA Cup trophy. What team did they defeat in the final?

    a. Middlesbrough ☐

    b. Southampton ☐

    c. Manchester City ☐

    d. Chelsea ☐

(ANSWERS CAN BE FOUND ON PAGE 86)

SECTION SIX

EURO 2000 ARSENAL PLAYERS

Nine Arsenal players were selected for their respective countries for Euro 2000. Can you name them all? (Initials and country given)

DS	ENGLAND	
TA	ENGLAND	
MK	ENGLAND	
FL	SWEDEN	
PV	FRANCE	
TH	FRANCE	
EP	FRANCE	
DB	NETHERLANDS	
MO	NETHERLANDS	

(ANSWERS CAN BE FOUND ON PAGE 87)

SECTION SEVEN

PREMIER LEAGUE YEARS
2004-2006

1. In January 2004 Arsenal signed Jose Antonio Reyes for a fee potentially rising to £17 million. Which Spanish club did he sign from?

    a. Malaga ☐

    b. Villareal ☐

    c. Sevilla ☐

    d. Espanyol ☐

2. The 2003-2004 season saw Arsenal win their 3rd Premier League title in their famous invincible season. Conceding just 26 goals in 38 games who was the Goalkeeper this season?

   a. David Seaman ☐

   b. Stuart Taylor ☐

   c. Graham Stack ☐

   d. Jens Lehmann ☐

3. May 2004 saw Arsenal signed Robin Van Persie from Feyenoord. How much did Arsenal pay for the player?

   a. £2.75 million ☐

   b. £5 million ☐

   c. £12.75 million ☐

   d. £17.5 million ☐

4. Arsenals Invincibles finally lost on 24th October 2004. Losing 2-0 at Old Trafford. How many games had Arsenal been undefeated?

    a. 38 ☐

    b. 45 ☐

    c. 49 ☐

    d. 51 ☐

5. On 14th February 2005 Arsenal became the first English club to name an entirely foreign matchday squad. The selection paid dividends with Arsenal running out 5-1 winners against which London club?

    a. Chelsea ☐

    b. Crystal Palace ☐

    c. Charlton Athletic ☐

    d. West Ham United ☐

6. The 2004-05 season saw Arsenal finish 2nd to Chelsea failing to win back-to-back titles. However, the season ended with more silverware as Arsenal won the FA cup against Manchester United. How did they win the trophy?

    a. 2-0 ☐

    b. 2-1 ☐

    c. 1-0 in Extra Time ☐

    d. 5-4 on Penalties ☐

7. Arsenal signed a 17-year-old French midfielder on 11th August 2005 initially on loan before later completing a permanent move. He went on to play over 200 games for the Gunners. Who was he?

    a. Abou Diaby ☐

    b. Alexander Hleb ☐

    c. Alex Song ☐

    d. Mathieu Flamini ☐

8. Arsenal recorded their biggest win of the season against Middlesbrough on 14th January 2006. Henry scored a hattrick and Reyes secured 4 assists. What was the final score?

    a. 5-0 ☐

    b. 6-1 ☐

    c. 7-0 ☐

    d. 8-2 ☐

9. On May 7th 2006 Arsenal played their last game at Highbury. With Henry scoring yet another hattrick. Who was the opponent that day in a 4-2 Arsenal victory?

    a. Southampton ☐

    b. Wigan Athletic ☐

    c. Newcastle United ☐

    d. West Bromwich Albion ☐

10. The 2005-06 season ended without silverware. But Arsenals notable run to the Champions League Final was the highlight. Unfortunately ending in a 2-1 defeat against Barcelona. Who scored Arsenals opening goal as they took the lead in the first half?

   a. Thierry Henry ☐

   b. Alexander Hleb ☐

   c. Sol Campbell ☐

   d. Robert Pires ☐

(ANSWERS CAN BE FOUND ON PAGE 88)

SECTION EIGHT

CROSSING THE DIVIDE

Clues to three players that have played for both Arsenal and Tottenham during the Premier League Era

1. A youth Arsenal product who made 9 appearances for Arsenal – just 1 in the Premier league. He went on to play 62 times for Tottenham after joining for a fee of £15 million in 2008.

    ┌─────────────────────────────────────┐
    │   │
    │   │
    └─────────────────────────────────────┘

2. This player signed for Arsenal from Chelsea in 2006. He made 142 appearances for Arsenal before joining Tottenham in 2010 playing 78 times.

    ┌─────────────────────────────────────┐
    │   │
    └─────────────────────────────────────┘

3. A signing from Monaco in 2005 scoring 62 times in 142 appearances for the Gunners. He departed to join Manchester City before arriving at White Hart Lane in 2011.

(ANSWERS CAN BE FOUND ON PAGE 89)

PREMIER LEAGUE YEARS
2007-2010

1. The 2006-2007 season was the first season Arsenal played at the Emirates. Against which team did Arsenal record their first league victory at the new stadium?

   a. Sheffield United ☐

   b. Charlton Athletic ☐

   c. Manchester United ☐

   d. Watford ☐

2. June 2007 saw Arsenal Legend Thierry Henry depart the club to join Barcelona. He finished with 175 league goals. But how many goals had he scored for Arsenal in total?

   a. 204 ☐

   b. 216 ☐

   c. 228 ☐

   d. 232 ☐

3. Following Henrys departure which Striker took up the goalscoring task and finished as the clubs top Premier League goalscorer with 24 goals?

   a. Cesc Fabregas ☐

   b. Robin Van Persie ☐

   c. Emmanuel Adebayor ☐

   d. Dennis Bergkamp ☐

4. The 2007-2008 season saw Arsenal change goalkeeper due to Jens Lehmann picking up an Achilles injury in August. What keeper played 29 league games this season and essentially became number 1 for the following two seasons?

    a. Manuel Almunia ☐

    b. Lukasz Fabianski ☐

    c. Vito Mannone ☐

    d. Wojciech Szczesny ☐

5. What midfielder signed for Arsenal from Marseille in July 2008? He went on to make 125 appearances in total for Arsenal before departing to join Manchester City in 2011.

    a. Gael Clichy ☐

    b. Abou Diaby ☐

    c. William Gallas ☐

    d. Samir Nasri ☐

6. On 24th November 2008 what player was named as Arsenals permanent captain following William Gallas being stripped of the Captaincy due to a verbal outburst against Arsenal players?

    a. Kolo Toure ☐

    b. Tomas Rosicky ☐

    c. Robin Van Persie ☐

    d. Cesc Fabregas ☐

7. What English club knocked Arsenal out of the Champions League in the Semi Finals played in April/May 2009 with a 4-1 aggregate defeat?

    a. Chelsea ☐

    b. Manchester United ☐

    c. Liverpool ☐

    d. Manchester City ☐

8. Who did Arsenal sign from Ajax for around £10 million on 19th June 2009 and took over the recently vacated number 5 jersey?

    a. Aaron Ramsey ☐

    b. Mikael Silvestre ☐

    c. Thomas Vermaelen ☐

    d. Philippe Senderos ☐

9. Who scored four goals at Anfield on 21st April 2009 in a thrilling 4-4 draw?

    a. Cesc Fabregas ☐

    b. Robin Van Persie ☐

    c. Carlos Vela ☐

    d. Andrey Arshavin ☐

10. Laurent Koscielny joined the club on 7th July 2010. He went on to play over 250 league games for Arsenal - what French club did Arsenal sign him from?

    a. Lorient ☐

    b. St Etienne ☐

    c. Toulouse ☐

    d. Brest ☐

(ANSWERS CAN BE FOUND ON PAGE 90)

YOUNG GUNS

Initials	Games	Years	Name
1. AI	100	2015-17	
2. HB	183	2012-21	
3. JW	125	2008-18	
4. BS	135	2018-	
5. EM	15	2011-21	
6. JW	40	2017-21	
7. AMN	72	2014-23	
8. EN	89	2017-	
9. RN	34	2017-	
10. ESR	67	2018-	

Above are Clues to Arsenal youth products that came through the academy since 1992 - initials, number of league games for the club and the years he played for the club are provided

(ANSWERS CAN BE FOUND ON PAGE 91)

PREMIER LEAGUE YEARS
2011-2013

1. On April 11th 2011 who increased his shareholdings in the club to 63% with the club valued at £731 million?

    a. Stan Kroenke ☐

    b. Danny Fiszman ☐

    c. Alisher Usmanov ☐

    d. Farhad Moshiri ☐

2. Cesc Fabregas left Arsenal in August 2011 after playing over 200 games for Arsenal. What club did he join for a reported £35 million?

   a. Chelsea ☐

   b. Barcelona ☐

   c. Real Madrid ☐

   d. Paris St Germain ☐

3. Arsenal signed Mikel Arteta from which club for a fee of £10 million in the same summer?

   a. Real Oviedo ☐

   b. Rangers ☐

   c. Everton ☐

   d. Real Sociedad ☐

4. Robin Van Persie finished as Arsenals top goalscorer in the 2011-2012 season for the 4th time. How many goals did he score in the Premier League?

    a. 20 ☐

    b. 25 ☐

    c. 30 ☐

    d. 35 ☐

5. Arsenal fell to a humbling defeat at Old Trafford on 28th August 2011. What was the final score?

    a. 6-0 ☐

    b. 6-2 ☐

    c. 7-1 ☐

    d. 8-2 ☐

6. Arsenal signed striker Lukas Podolski from which German club in April 2012?

    a. RB Leipzig ☐

    b. VfB Stuttgart ☐

    c. FC Koln ☐

    d. Bayer Leverkusen ☐

7. Later in the close season Arsenal signed a striker from Montpellier for £12.8 million. He scored 105 goals in 253 appearances for Arsenal. What was his name?

    a. Gervinho ☐

    b. Marouane Chamakh ☐

    c. Olivier Giroud ☐

    d. Joel Campbell ☐

8. 29ᵗʰ December saw Arsenal run out as 7-3 winners – the joint highest scoring game in the Premier League – who were their opponents?

    a. Leicester City ☐

    b. Newcastle United ☐

    c. Southampton ☐

    d. Leeds United ☐

9. The January transfer window of 2013 saw which Spanish player join the club from Malaga?

    a. Hector Bellerin ☐

    b. Carlos Vela ☐

    c. Nacho Monreal ☐

    d. Alex Song ☐

10. The 2012-13 season saw an English player finish as Arsenals top league goalscorer for the first time since Ian Wright nearly 20 years prior. Who achieved this?

    a. Jack Wilshere ☐

    b. Alex Oxlade-Chamberlain ☐

    c. Aaron Ramsey ☐

    d. Theo Walcott ☐

(ANSWERS CAN BE FOUND ON PAGE 92)

2014 FA CUP WINNING XI

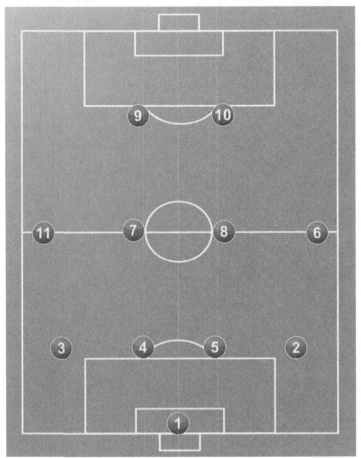

(The numbers used are to represent positions only – they are not accurate as worn on the day)

How many of the Arsenal 2014 FA CUP XI final winners can you name?

1. LF	
2. BS	
3. KG	
4. PM	
5. LK	
6. AR	
7. SC	
8. MA	
9. LP	
10. MO	
11. OG	

(ANSWERS CAN BE FOUND ON PAGE 93)

SECTION THIRTEEN

PREMIER LEAGUE YEARS 2014-2016

1. Arsenal unveiled a statue of which legend in February 2014? The statue depicts the player in Action against Newcastle in 2003

    a. Thierry Henry ☐

    b. Patrick Vieira ☐

    c. Dennis Bergkamp ☐

    d. Robert Pires ☐

2. Arsenal won the FA Cup on 17th May 2014 ending a trophy drought that stretched back how many years?

   a. 5 ☐

   b. 6 ☐

   c. 8 ☐

   d. 9 ☐

3. Who did Arsenal defeat in the 2014 cup final at Wembley after extra time?

   a. Birmingham City ☐

   b. Wigan Athletic ☐

   c. Leicester City ☐

   d. Hull City ☐

4. And who scored the winning Extra Time goal after 109 minutes?

   a. Santi Cazorla ☐

   b. Olivier Giroud ☐

   c. Bacary Sagna ☐

   d. Aaron Ramsey ☐

5. On 10th July 2014 Arsenal signed a player from Barcelona for a fee of £31.7 million. He went on to score 80 goals in 166 games – who is the player?

   a. Mesut Ozil ☐

   b. Alexis Sanchez ☐

   c. Henrikh Mkhitaryan ☐

   d. Lucas Perez ☐

6. August 2014 saw Arsenal win the community shield with an impressive 3-0 victory. What title holders did they defeat?

   a. Manchester United ☐

   b. Liverpool ☐

   c. Chelsea ☐

   d. Manchester City ☐

7. In the summer transfer window Arsenal spent £16 million on Danny Welbeck – from which club did he sign?

    a. West Ham United ☐

    b. Wigan Athletic ☐

    c. Manchester United ☐

    d. Leeds United ☐

8. Arsenal went back-to-back winning the FA Cup again in 2015. Defeating Aston Villa at Wembley – what was the final score?

    a. 1-0 ☐

    b. 2-1 AET ☐

    c. 5-3 on Penalties ☐

    d. 4-0 ☐

9. What player did Arsenal sign from Chelsea in June 2015 for a fee of £10 million? He spent 4 seasons at Arsenal playing 139 games

  a. Calum Chambers ☐

  b. Mathieu Debuchy ☐

  c. Petr Cech ☐

  d. David Luiz ☐

10. The 2015-16 season saw Arsenal finish 2nd in the league 10 points behind which Champions?

  a. Leicester City ☐

  b. Liverpool ☐

  c. Chelsea ☐

  d. Manchester United ☐

(ANSWERS CAN BE FOUND ON PAGE 94)

THE FRENCH REVOLUTION

Top 12 French appearances makers for arsenal

1. PV	400 GAMES	
2. TH	376 GAMES	
3. LK	353 GAMES	
4. RP	284 GAMES	
5. BS	284 GAMES	
6. GC	264 GAMES	
7. OG	253 GAMES	
8. MF	246 GAMES	
9. AL	206 GAMES	
10. AD	180 GAMES	
11. SW	175 GAMES	
12. GG	165 GAMES	

(ANSWERS CAN BE FOUND ON PAGE 95)

SECTION FIFTEEN

PREMIER LEAGUE YEARS
2017-2019

1. On New Year's Day 2017 which player scored a 'Scorpion kick' in a 2-0 win over Crystal Palace?

    a. Danny Welbeck ☐

    b. Jack Wilshere ☐

    c. Olivier Giroud ☐

    d. Theo Walcott ☐

2. The Quarter final of the FA cup saw Arsenal draw the last remaining non-league team in the competition. Arsenal went on to win 5-0 in March against which team?

    a. Sutton United ☐

    b. Wrexham ☐

    c. Oxford United ☐

    d. Lincoln City ☐

3. Following the Quarter Final victory Arsenal beat Manchester City 2-1 in the Semi-finals leading to a final - with Arsenal lifting the cup against which club?

    a. Manchester United ☐

    b. Reading ☐

    c. Brighton and Hove Albion ☐

    d. Chelsea ☐

4. What player scored 30 goals in all competitions to finish as Arsenals top goalscorer in the 2016-17 season?

   a. Alexis Sanchez ☐

   b. Theo Walcott ☐

   c. Olivier Giroud ☐

   d. Mesut Ozil ☐

5. Arsenal broke their transfer record when they signed which player from Lyon for a fee in excess of £45 million in July 2017?

   a. Granit Xhaka ☐

   b. Alexandre Lacazette ☐

   c. Pierre Emerick-Aubameyang ☐

   d. Lucas Torreira ☐

6. What English player left to join Liverpool for £35 million during the same window?

    a. Kieran Gibbs ☐

    b. Theo Walcott ☐

    c. Alex Oxlade-Chamberlain ☐

    d. Jack Wilshere ☐

7. Arsene Wenger announced in April 2018 that he would be departing the club at the end of the season after 22 years at Arsenal. How many major trophies did he win during this spell?

    a. 5 ☐

    b. 8 ☐

    c. 10 ☐

    d. 14 ☐

8. Unai Emery was appointed Arsenal manager after Wenger's departure. Who had he managed immediately prior to joining Arsenal?

    a. Paris Saint Germain ☐

    b. Villareal ☐

    c. Valencia ☐

    d. Real Madrid ☐

9. The 2018-19 season saw Arsenal finish 5th in the league. However, Emery had previously lifted the Europa League on three occasions and hoped to make it four with Arsenal. Unfortunately losing out 4-1 to which club in the Final in Baku?

    a. Chelsea ☐

    b. Atletico Madrid ☐

    c. Sevilla ☐

    d. Inter Milan ☐

10. A disappointing start to the 2019-20 campaign saw Emery lose his job in November. Which former Arsenal star took his place on an interim basis?

    a. Tony Adams ☐

    b. Steve Bould ☐

    c. Freddie Ljungberg ☐

    d. Robert Pires ☐

(ANSWERS CAN BE FOUND ON PAGE 96)

SECTION SIXTEEN

ARSENAL 2020 FA CUP WINNING XI

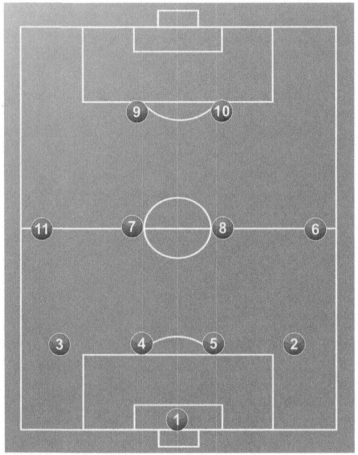

(The numbers used are to represent positions only – they are not accurate as worn on the day)

How many of the Arsenal 2020 FA CUP XI final winners can you name?

1. EM	
2. HB	
3. KT	
4. DL	
5. RH	
6. GX	
7. NP	
8. DC	
9. AL	
10. PEA	
11. AMN	

(ANSWERS CAN BE FOUND ON PAGE (97)

PREMIER LEAGUE YEARS
2020-2023

1. On 1st January 2020 new permanent manager Mikel Arteta got his first victory in a 2-0 win over which club?

    a. Manchester United ☐

    b. West Bromwich Albion ☐

    c. Southampton ☐

    d. AFC Bournemouth ☐

2. In May 2020 with the COVID-19 pandemic meaning the game had to be played behind closed doors Arsenal won their first silverware under Arteta. Defeating Chelsea 2-1 in the FA Cup Final which player scored both goals??

   a. Nicolas Pepe ☐

   b. Alexandre Lacazette ☐

   c. Granit Xhaka ☐

   d. Pierre-Emerick Aubameyang ☐

3. Who did Arsenal sell to Aston Villa in September 2020 for a fee of £20 million?

   a. Kieran Gibbs ☐

   b. Calum Chambers ☐

   c. Emiliano Martinez ☐

   d. Joe Willock ☐

4. Arsenal purchased which player for £45 million in 2020 from Atletico Madrid?

   a. Gabriel Martinelli ☐

   b. Martin Odegaard ☐

   c. William Saliba ☐

   d. Thomas Partey ☐

5. The 2020-21 season was Mikel Artetas first full season in charge. Finishing 8th and failing to win any silverware meant their first season without European football for how long?

   a. 16 years ☐

   b. 22 years ☐

   c. 27 years ☐

   d. 30 years ☐

6. 11th July 2021 saw the Euro 2000 final played (a year late due to COVID-19) The Italians beating England on penalties to lift the trophy. How many Arsenal players featured in the England squad?

    a. 1 ☐

    b. 2 ☐

    c. 3 ☐

    d. 4 ☐

7. 2021-22 saw the season recorded for a documentary to be aired on Amazon Prime Video – what was the documentary called?

    a. All in All ☐

    b. All or Nothing ☐

    c. Now or Never ☐

    d. Winning is Everything ☐

8. 2021-22 ended as a disappointing season - Arsenal finished 5th losing out to rivals Tottenham to a Champions League spot. What club did Arsenal beat 5-1 on the last day of the season in vain?

   a. Leeds United ☐

   b. West Ham United☐

   c. Newcastle United ☐

   d. Crystal Palace ☐

9. July 2022 saw Arsenal raid Artetas former club Manchester City and sign Gabriel Jesus and Oleksander Zinchenko – what was the combined fee for the pair?

   a. £45 million ☐

   b. £55 million ☐

   c. £65 million ☐

   d. £75 million ☐

10. 2022/23 ended somewhat disappointingly as Arsenal lost out on the title to a Manchester City team that went on to win the treble. However, Arsenal were back to their best and had a terrific season – how many days did they spend at the top of the Premier League?

    a. 205 ☐

    b. 218 ☐

    c. 248 ☐

    d. 265 ☐

(ANSWERS CAN BE FOUND ON PAGE 98)

ANSWERS

Section 1: Premier League years 1992-1995

1. B – George Graham

2. C – Martin Keown

3. A – Steve Morrow

4. D – 2-1

5. C - 30

6. A - Parma

7. C – Anders Limpar

8. A – Luton Town

9. C – Ian Wright

10. B - Nayim

/10

ANSWERS

Section two: Name the famous Gooners

1. David Platt

2. David O'leary

3. Ray Parlour

4. Jack Wilshere

5. Andrey Arshavin

6. Nicolas Anelka

7. Ashley Cole

8. Gael Clichy

9. Theo Walcott

10. Sol Campbell

/10

ANSWERS

Section Three: 1993 FA Cup winning starting XI

1. DS   David Seaman

2. LD   Lee Dixon

3. NW   Nigel Winterburn

4. AL   Andy Linighan

5. TA   Tony Adams

6. PD   Paul Davis

7. JJ   John Jensen

8. IW   Ian Wright

9. KC   Kevin Campbell

10. PM   Paul Merson

11. RP   Ray Parlour

/11

ANSWERS

Section four: Premier League Years 1996-1999

1. D – John Lukic

2. A - Monaco

3. B – Patrick Vieira and Remi Garde

4. A - 1

5. B - Ajax

6. D – Newcastle United

7. A – Freddie Ljungberg

8. B – Inter Milan

9. C – Nicholas Anelka

10. D – Manchester United

/10

ANSWERS

Section Five: Premier League Years 2000-2003

1. C - 17

2. B – Runners Up

3. A - Barcelona

4. B - 8

5. D – Francis Jeffers

6. B – Premier League and FA Cup

7. A – Lee Dixon

8. C – Freddie Ljungberg

9. D – Gilberto Silva

10. B – Southampton

/10

ANSWERS

Section six: Euro 2000 Arsenal Players

1. DS – David Seaman

2. TA – Tony Adams

3. MK – Martin Keown

4. FL – Freddie Ljungberg

5. PV – Patrick Vieira

6. TH – Thierry Henry

7. EP – Emmanuel Petit

8. DB – Dennis Bergkamp

9. MO – Marc Overmars

/9

ANSWERS

Section seven: Premier League Years 2004-2006

1. C - Sevilla

2. D – Jens Lehmann

3. A - £2.75 million

4. C - 49

5. B – Crystal Palace

6. D – 5-4 on Penalties

7. C – Alex Song

8. C – 7-0

9. B – Wigan Athletic

10. C – Sol Campbell

/10

ANSWERS

Section eight: Crossing the Divide

1. David Bentley

2. William Gallas

3. Emmanuel Adebayor

/3

ANSWERS

Section nine: Premier League Years 2007-2010

1. A – Sheffield United

2. C - 228

3. C – Emmanuel Adebayor

4. A – Manuel Almunia

5. D – Samir Nasri

6. D – Cesc Fabregas

7. B – Manchester United

8. C – Thomas Vermaelen

9. D – Andrey Arshavin

10. A - Lorient

/10

ANSWERS

Section Ten: Young Guns

1. Alex Iwobi

2. Hector Bellerin

3. Jack Wilshere

4. Bukayo Saka

5. Emi Martinez

6. Joe Willock

7. Ainsley Maitland Niles

8. Eddie Nketiah

9. Reiss Nelson

10. Emile Smith Rowe

/10

ANSWERS

Section Eleven: Premier League Years 2011-2013

1. A – Stan Kroenke

2. B - Barcelona

3. C - Everton

4. C - 30

5. D – 8-2

6. C – FC Koln

7. C – Olivier Giroud

8. B – Newcastle United

9. C – Nacho Monreal

10. D – Theo Walcott

/10

ANSWERS

Section Twelve: Arsenal 2014 FA CUP final XI

1.	LF	Lukasz Fabianski
2.	BS	Bacary Sagna
3.	KG	Kieron Gibbs
4.	PM	Per Mertesacker
5.	LK	Laurent Koscielny
6.	AR	Aaron Ramsey
7.	SC	Santi Cazorla
8.	MA	Mikel Arteta
9.	LP	Lukas Podolski
10.	MO	Mesut Ozil
11.	OG	Olivier Giroud

/11

ANSWERS

Section Thirteen: Premier League Years 2014-2016

1. C – Dennis Bergkamp

2. C – 8 years

3. D – Hull City

4. D – Aaron Ramsey

5. B – Alexis Sanchez

6. D – Manchester City

7. C – Manchester United

8. D – 4-0

9. C – Petr Cech

10. A – Leicester City

/10

ANSWERS

Section Fourteen: The French Revolution

1. PV	Patrick Vieira
2. TH	Thierry Henry
3. LK	Laurent Koscielny
4. RP	Robert Pires
5. BS	Bacary Sagna
6. GC	Gael Clichy
7. OG	Olivier Giroud
8. MF	Mathieu Flamini
9. AL	Alexandre Lacazette
10. AD	Abou Diaby
11. SW	Silvain Wiltord
12. GG	Gilles Grimandi

/12

ANSWERS

Section Fifteen: Premier League years 2017-2019

1. C – Olivier Giroud

2. D – Lincoln City

3. D - Chelsea

4. A – Alexis Sanchez

5. B – Alexandre Lacazette

6. C – Alex Oxlade-Chamberlain

7. B - 8

8. A – Paris Saint Germain

9. A - Chelsea

10. C – Freddie Ljungberg

/10

ANSWERS

Section Sixteen: Arsenal 2020 FA Cup Starting XI

1. Emiliano Martinez
2. Hector Bellerin
3. Kieran Tierney
4. David Luiz
5. Rob Holding
6. Granit Xhaka
7. Nicolas Pepe
8. Dani Ceballos
9. Alexandre Lacazette
10. Pierre-Emerick Aubameyang
11. Ainsley Maitland Niles

/11

ANSWERS

Section Seventeen: Premier League Years 2020-2023

1. A – Manchester United

2. D – Pierre-Emerick Aubameyang

3. C – Emiliano Martinez

4. D – Thomas Partey

5. C – 27 years

6. A – 1 (Saka)

7. B – All or Nothing

8. C – Newcastle United

9. D - £75 million

10. C - 248 days

/10

That completes the quiz and with a total of 167 points available – where do you stand?

150-167 True Gooner

125-149 Remarkable Red

101-124 North London and Proud

51-100 Room for Improvement

26-50 Still learning the ropes

0-25 Are you a Spurs Fan in disguise???

Hopefully you have enjoyed this little quiz book and it has been a challenge but your knowledge has extended and been rewarded. Now it's time to challenge your friends and family. Challenge the ardent fan that claims they know everything and see whether they are a True Gooner or a closet Spurs.

Take away multiple choice options for the easier questions and use the book to teach the next generation of fans about the history of this great club.

Arsenal Stats and Records

The following pages provide all time stats and records for Arsenal Football Club.

Most Appearances (as a sub)

1. David O'leary 722 (14)
2. Tony Adams 669 (48)
3. George Armstrong 621 (68)
4. Lee Dixon 619 (28)
5. Nigel Winterburn 584 (12)
6. David Seaman 564 (0)
7. Pat Rice 528 (13)
8. Peter Storey 501 (17)
9. John Radford 481 (149)
10. Peter Simpson 477 (15)

Top Goalscorers

1. Thierry Henry 228
2. Ian Wright 185
3. Cliff Bastin 178
4. John Radford 149
5. Jimmy Brain 139
6. Ted Drake 139
7. Doug Lishman 137
8. Robin Van Persie 132
9. Joe Hulme 125
10. David Jack 124

Record Transfer fees paid

1. Declan Rice £100 million
2. Nicolas Pepe £72 million
3. Kai Havertz £65 million
4. Pierre-Emerick Aubameyang £56 million
5. Ben White £50 million
6. Alexandre Lacazette £46.5 million
7. Thomas Partey £45.3 million
8. Gabriel Jesus £45 million
9. Mesut Ozil £42.4 million
10. Shkodran Mustafi, Alexis Sanchez, Grant Xhaka £35 million

Highest Transfer fees received

1. Alex Oxlaide-Chamberlain £35 million
2. Alex Iwobi £28 million
3. Cesc Fabregas £25.4 million
4. Emmanuel Adebayor £25 million
5. Samir Nasri £25 million
6. Marc Overmars £25 million
7. Nicolas Anelka £23.5 million
8. Robin Van Persie £22.5 million
9. Granit Xhaka £21.4 million
10. Joe Willock £20 million

Trophies

First Division and Premier League titles

Winners(13):

1930–31,

1932–33,

1933–34,

1934–35,

1937–38,

1947–48,

1952–53,

1970–71,

1988–89,

1990–91,

1997–98,

2001–02,

2003–04

EFL Cup

Winners (2):

1986–87,

1992-93

FA Cup

Winners(14):
1929–30,
1935–36,
1949–50,
1970–71,
1978–79,
1992–93,
1997–98,
2001–02,
2002–03,
2004–05,
2013–14,
2014–15,
2016–17,
2019–20

UEFA Cup Winners Cup
Winners (1)
1993-94

Most goals in a season :
Ted Drake (44) 1934-35

Most goals in a match :
Ted Drake (7) v Aston Villa 14 December 1935

Most league goals in a 38 game season :
Thierry Henry (30) 2003-04
Robin Van Persie (30) 2011-12

Youngest Goalscorer :
Cesc Fabregas 16 years 212 days v Wolves 2 Dec 2003

Youngest Hattrick scorer :
John Radford 17 years 315 days v Wolves 2 Jan 1965

Most league appearances :
David O'leary 558

Most FA Cup appearances :
David O'leary 70

Most European appearances
Thierry Henry 86

Printed in Great Britain
by Amazon

34197376R00066